WHY DIDN'T ANYONE TELL US?

What We Didn't Know About Attachment Disorder

Lynn Pike

ISBN: 978-0-692-26433-1
ISBN-978-0-692-26433-1

PUBLISHED BY LYNN PIKE
THIS BOOK IS NOT INTENDED TO
DIAGNOSE OR TREAT ILLNESSES.
EVERYONE'S SITUATION IS DIFFERENT.
CONSULT A LICENSED THREAPIST,
PSYCHOTHERAPIST OR A PHYSICIAN FOR
YOUR INDIVIDUAL NEEDS. THIS BOOK IS
WRITEN TO TELL YOU OUR EXPERIENCE
FOR YOUR INFORMATION AND
ENCOURAGEMENT.

CONTENTS

Contents

INTRODUCTION

My purpose for writing this book is to tell our story and encourage other parents who may be going through a similar situation to seek help early, early, early in a child's life. We did not understand what was happening at the time or what to do about it, until it was too late. Of all the counselors and physicians we have seen over the years no one addressed the oppositional defiance.

I don't want to discourage anyone from adopting, but go into it knowing that "love is not enough". Know the signs of Reactive Attachment Disorder and be aggressive in getting what help you can find. If your child has any of these signs head straight to a good psychotherapist.

1- ON HIS OWN

November 1999 the social worker brought Andy to our home with a small plastic bag of clothes, and a three-week-old antibiotic prescription for his ear infection. He had a fever, runny nose, did not make eye contact, and was thin. I took his prescription to the pharmacy that day, brought it home and started him on the antibiotics. He had been in his first foster home three months earlier. Since he was not being cared for, and they had too many children, the social worker called other foster homes trying to find another place for Andy. Then they called us.

Andy was two. He had a Guardian Ad Litem who was assigned to him at birth, because he was an *at risk* baby. His birth mom was 19. She had one other child who was adopted out privately to a couple through a lawyer, and a set of twins less than two years older than Andy. The twins were in the custody of her mother. For some reason, she decided to keep Andy. I think he was her only boy. His Guardian Ad Litem had been following him and his birth mom for two years. She tried to help his birth mom take care of him, but she would not cooperate. She had been abused as a child herself. The birth mom's mother called the Department of Social Services, because she did not take care of Andy. The birth mom watched TV all day while Andy just walked around and did whatever he wanted. She did not take him outside for a walk or to the park. She didn't have any books for him in her apartment she shared with her boyfriend. Andy's birth dad was in prison. We did not know why. Andy was *on his own during his first years.*

Andy's first night in our home he cried, "Mama, Mama." My heart ached for him. Every night I would hold him, sing to him, and pray for him until he fell asleep. He slept all night his first time here, and thereafter. I was thankful for that. He started calling me Mom. As stressful as he was during the day, it was a blessing to be able to sleep at night.

Andy had visitations with his birth mom, grandmother, and twin sisters once a week. Visitations went on for almost a year after which the courts took her rights away, because she was non-compliant to everything she was told, such as getting a job, a permanent place to live, and parenting classes. She was living in a hotel room.

After her rights were taken away, we knew we

wanted to adopt Andy. His birth mom refused to give us any baby pictures of Andy. I wanted him to have some since our other children would have theirs. The adoption took about 10 months to complete. In August 2001 Andy was officially our son. We were so excited. He had a new Social Security card and a birth certificate with our last name on them. We had decided to let him know he was adopted, but no other facts till he started asking more questions. He wouldn't understand what adoption meant until he was older. We decided to always be honest and upfront with him.

My husband, John, and I had always talked about adopting a child. In the beginning we thought we would prefer a baby. We took foster parenting classes thinking we would have a baby around to "kinda" test the waters. Adopting a foster child cost much less money than other adoptions. We only had to pay $40 for adoption fees. The county paid the rest.

The number of infants needing foster care has decreased in recent years. We were told it was a result of private adoptions at birth, mothers keeping their children, and abortions. Our first call to foster parent was for a 13 year old girl who was sexually abused. We said no because we were concerned about our nine year old son. I was working part time and homeschooling three children, when they called us, to keep a child who needed 24 hour care since she was physically disabled. It was hard to say no, but I know my limits. Then we were called about Andy. He fit more with our family. We accepted him before seeing him. We were amazed how much he looked like he belonged in our family with blue eyes and blonde hair.

Little did we know our home would never be the same again.

I felt as though I could not take the time to breathe. Every second of Andy's awake time, I would have to be in a state of heightened awareness. He was always trying to go out doors. I felt so bad for him. He didn't know any better and has seen much more than a little boy or girl should ever have to see or experience.

He couldn't sit and play alone or with me for much longer than five minutes. He was compelled to get up and wander. If we went to someone's house, he took off to look through the house without stopping. He wasn't afraid of strangers. He would go up to anyone.

He didn't listen to anything we said to him. We expected some of this, but didn't realize just how difficult it would be to discipline a toddler who had never been disciplined till now. We had to watch him like a hawk. He would be gone in a second. I was never sure what he was looking for. I don't think he knew either.

It is amazing how much a newborn learns in the first two years of life, or doesn't learn. That time is so crucial to bonding and learning to love.

Andy was opposite of our other three biological children who were still living at home. We didn't have experience with this type of personality. They were easy going and somewhat laid back. Andy was not at all. Our oldest child, Lynn, loved Andy. She was around 16 and willingly helped in the evenings to watch him when I went to work at the hospital on the 3-11 shift. My husband came home around 6 or 7 PM.

One evening I had gone to my Jazzercise class from 6-7 PM. When I returned home, my husband was outside working, and our two older boys were outside playing baseball. Our daughter was gone. I didn't see Andy. I asked my husband if he knew where he was. He said he was with our other boys. When I asked the boys, they said he was with Dad. I was worried. We looked in the house and around our three acres of land. No Andy. I called 911. In minutes there were five deputy cars at our house. We had neighbors helping look, too.

I was crying and worried he may have to stay out all night alone. Just as the deputies were getting ready to bring in sniffing dogs, a neighbor found him. He was in a nearby cow field, with cows close to him. There were several acres of woods separating our yard to this field. Not sure why he would just keep walking and walking where big animals were. At two years old he wasn't afraid of anything. He wasn't even crying when he was found. We were so relieved.

Andy always wants attention. When I say always that is precisely what I mean. He was very jealous of our son Caleb who was nine when we adopted Andy. They never got along or liked each other. It saddened me tremendously. Andy was constantly aggravating Caleb to get Caleb's attention. We tried many ways to bring them closer together.

As Caleb grew older, he made a point to stay away from wherever Andy was, even if it meant not being at home. Those years were very difficult. Caleb suffered because Andy demanded all of our time and attention. If he didn't have what he wanted, he got it in anyway he could. He was always good at pushing my buttons, and even pushing buttons I didn't know I had. This upset Caleb. Caleb and I had always had a wonderful relationship. He did not like to see me stressed all the time.

I was not always in control of my emotions. Andy did not respond to discipline or punishment. He didn't show any remorse when he had done something we had told him not to do, such as taking someone's things without asking. This was a big issue. As he grew older, four, five, and six, his stealing and lying increased. We couldn't seem to impress that these things were wrong.

I talk about how Andy was always seeking attention. We gave him lots of attention. He liked to play board games with us until he reached 15. His brothers would get upset, because Andy always cheated, and would not listen to instructions. So they didn't want to play with him. We went to parks, camping, science centers, etc. Even though he had lots of attention, it seemed not to be enough.

It was exhausting on me to try to do anything else. I felt constantly in a state of flight or fight when he was close by, because I never knew what the next crisis would be. The only time I could breathe was if I knew he was away safe with someone I trusted, or buckled in his car seat. I used to go out a lot just to have a break with him in his car seat and out of trouble. We took him and Caleb to the YMCA a lot. We didn't have very much help or support from others, except a few friends and my Mom.

My Mom would take care of Andy sometimes for me, but by the end of the day, she was frustrated. He would walk out of her house, without her knowing, head down our street, and stay gone for 30 or 40 minutes. She would be so frantic and worried. Usually he would go to a friend's house in the neighborhood. I eventually had to give her our neighbors' phone numbers.

By the way, we have the best neighbors. They have been patient with Andy going to their house all the time, because he was bored most of the time. My Mom was in her upper 60s and couldn't go walking up and down the street looking for him.

He did not ask anyone if he could go next door or down the street. He wanted to be the person in charge. It was a struggle to get him to learn to ask permission. I explained to him we needed to know where he was and why. No matter how much we put him in time out, or talked to him, took things away, he continued to do this to her. I would hold my breath when I asked her how Andy was doing. She usually had a long list. I worked fewer hours, so she didn't have to watch him as much. It's sounds as though there wasn't any praise or love toward Andy, but my Mom loves him very much and still does. She prays for him constantly.

I did not know at the time that Andy's wanting to be in charge, was one characteristic of RAD (Reactive Attachment Disorder). RAD usually results when a newborn does not bond or attach to his birth Mom or other caregiver. Humans need this to learn to love, be loved, and to trust. The lying, stealing, showing no remorse, and needing constant stimulation were all indications, too. I wish I had known all this, and was able to find specific help.

We searched for some counseling for Andy and Caleb. By this time our older two teenagers had moved out and were on their own. When Andy was six, we took him to counseling. Caleb went a couple times, but he didn't want to. Caleb was 13 at this time. The counselor suggested Andy take medication for a while. He said Andy had all the symptoms of ADHD. That was all he said.

We tried different medications, and found one that was helpful to get him through school, but it made him less hungry. We never found just the right one. The only way he would sit still was if he was watching TV or playing a video game. Those two things would quickly become addictions. While on the medication he could sit still better, but he lost weight.

2- NO FEAR

Andy decided to slide down our laundry chute. It was from his upstairs bathroom to our basement. Not sure why. It may have been just because he thought about it. He made it all the way. We were all laughing when we found out. My husband was in the basement at the time, and was surprised he did it. If he had gotten stuck it would have been bad. My husband John would have had to tear into the wall near him. Andy didn't think about being afraid of getting stuck. He was four or five years old. Don't remember exact age.

Another time Andy went outside after everyone else had gone to sleep. Our doorknobs open from the inside even if they are locked. He opened the door, went out on our porch and closed it. The door was locked. He wasn't afraid of the dark. He laid down on our porch swing and went to sleep. He was around five. Later in the early morning hours we heard crying outside under our upstairs window. We thought it was a cat. We kept listening, but not able to figure out what it was, because we never thought Andy would be outside. My husband John got up to check. He walked out and saw Andy. Andy had walked around to the back of the house trying to get back in, but the doors were locked.

When Andy turned 10, we took him to the ADHD clinic associated with a local university. The results from extensive testing said he was attention deficit, hyperactive, plus he had what was called Oppositional Defiant Disorder. I could have told them all of this. Andy certainly has always opposed everything we would say or tell him to do. He did not like being told what to do. He wanted to be his own boss.

During the visitations with his birth mom, for his first year with us, she just followed Andy as he wandered around letting him do what he wanted, laughing, but no discipline or instructions. When I use the word "discipline" it means instruction, teaching, learning about things happening in our day, and how we could make it better.

Andy's ADHD & ODD has certain characteristics. Some are well known, such as short attention span, can't sit still, and needing constant stimulation. He sure wanted the constant stimulation. I didn't understand why. He still craves it.

The ODD comes in with his constant pushing of

my buttons, opposing authority, needing stimulation, lacking in social skills, or not listening to instructions. He is not happy till I, or anyone in authority become irritated, frustrated, and argues back with him. He did this in school, also. He could learn, but didn't want to put any effort in it. At school he wanted to be first to complete his seatwork. He would turn his paper in uncompleted, or all wrong answers just to be first.

At school Andy would pick on weaker kids, because he did not like anyone weaker or confrontational. He would criticize that person and call them a loser.

When he was in second grade, there was a shy little girl he picked on till she cried. We talked to him, grounded him, deprived him of TV, but it didn't help. Another time, a parent had come to class to read a story to the kids. Andy got behind the parent and started making rude gestures. I was so hurt. He didn't show any remorse. He seemed to be happy with himself, even when he hurt someone else. He was earning a negative reputation.

Before fifth grade started, there was a new

charter school being built near us. I thought this could be a new start for Andy to possibly make some new friends and enjoy school. We were positive and encouraged Andy. It was called Math and Science Academy. He liked math and science. We registered him and switched schools. The principal was Turkish, as well as the vice principal, and so was Andy's math teacher. Their accents were strong. They planned to teach the Turkish language to the kids. That was cool. Who teaches Turkish these days?

Classes got off to a good start. I was involved by helping with various projects at the school. Within weeks I began to get calls from the school, about Andy being disruptive in class, flying paper airplanes and not paying attention. Almost everyday I was called.

Andy was not bringing homework home. For a while I thought the teachers just didn't give it out. Silly me, I should have known better. I met with the principal, to ask if I could get Andy's assignments sent to me via email, because Andy threw any notes or assignments from teachers away before arriving home. The Principal would say they didn't have the system up yet.

I talked to his math teacher, because Andy could not understand him, and Andy was sitting at the back of the room. I told him he has trouble paying attention, and that he was diagnosed with ADHD. The teacher did not seem to know what ADHD was. They looked at me in a puzzled way. At the end of the grading period, Andy had zeros. I took him out of that school and put him back into the private Christian school, even though he didn't want to. They loved the children and watched them closely. The classrooms were smaller, plus they spoke clear English. When I tried to explain to Andy why we switched back, he never acknowledged any understanding. They helped him catch up, and pass fifth grade. Thank you God.

I will have to say, there have been a few times I explained something to Andy, and I saw the light bulb go off. He has a good memory. Although these days he only remembers the times someone has wronged him or perceives them as wrongs.

3- WHY DIDN'T ANYONE

TELL US

Counselors, physicians, and the ADHD clinic, never addressed the ODD side of Andy. It was always the popular ADHD. Oppositional disorder is serious if it doesn't get addressed and worked on early. It can grow into other social disorders. I have learned this in the past year, through research. Maybe it was still so new they didn't have much research on the outcomes 13 years ago. There are many new medications being approved by the FDA all the time. If your child has social disorders with ADHD and is very oppositional ask your primary physician if they can recommend a psychotherapist. Learn about the therapist as much as possible. Currently there is not a test to specifically diagnose psychopath, but there are guidelines for RAD in children under 18.

During Andy's extensive testing at the ADHD clinic in our town I received a copy of a checklist called, a Child Attachment Checklist, to fill out for him. The same checklist was sent to his sixth grade teacher to fill out. Our answers and hers were close to the same.

We didn't learn what to do about the answers. They had us fill it out and give it to them. That's it. Andy's symptoms were rated as severe on 23 out of 28. The other five answers were in the moderate level.

Many writings I have read say there is no cure for when a child never learns to bond, or attach to their mother or other caregiver. It's possible to get some therapy and use medication to help, but it doesn't cure it. There is a book by an author who went through detachment syndrome: *Detached: Surviving Reactive Attachment Disorder* by Jessie Hogsett, Kindle eBook on Amazon.com

When Andy was 13, our oldest daughter, her husband, and two-year-old daughter had to stay with us for six months. Andy really acted out. He was jealous they took some of his attention away.

One day he decided to climb out on the roof, walk over to the room our daughter and family were using, and peek in when they were getting ready for bed. She saw him and told us. We were very disappointed and upset he would do that.

Trying to explain to him why it's wrong didn't

seem to affect him. He never showed remorse. Later in the year, I found a black bra in his bedroom. I think it was my daughter's. She is a beautiful blonde. It bothers me he would have been disrespectful to his sister, or anyone else for that matter. She loved Andy and has always spent time with him and listened to him. Also her husband was very upset.

I don't know what is going on in Andy's head. He has never been able to tell us. Words are hard for him. I try to help him find the words, but he doesn't respond or try, he just gets angry.

He would not tell us, or could not, why he was using a plastic knife to cut on his lower arms. He would make several small cuts on his arms in school during class. They would bleed. A couple of times they became infected. I tried to tell him to clean the areas, put an antibacterial cream on, and stop cutting but he refused. This went on about a year, then he just finally stopped.

I've read self-cutting is a form of stimulation. A RAD or psychopath, have a need for self stimulation. They will cut, because it distracts them from other feelings or they will do other crazy things to get a buzz.

He was becoming interested in the opposite sex. He would look at magazines, every chance he got in the grocery stores, pharmacies, newspaper undergarment advertisements, etc. A boy at school showed him pornography. This was the ultimate stimulation for him. As much as I had tried to protect him from this before, I thought he could handle it. I feared it would do to him what it has done.

He was addicted. He would get it anyway he could. If we let him have time on our computer and I happened to step out of the room for a minute, he would jump to a nudity site in a second. I would come back, and he would get off. We checked the history before he learned how to delete it. John explained why it was harmful, disrespectful to girls, and wrong in God's eyes. No amount of talking has helped.

When I grounded him from using the computer, he would be angry and try to get back at me by purposefully making sarcastic remarks about our granddaughter or Caleb. He would also say bad things about anything I cared about, such as God, family, the small business I had, or just make personal attacks against me. He would ask to use our cell phones, for something innocent, then when we turned an eye for a second he was back on the porn.

We put passwords on everything. If one of our adult children were over, they would get Andy on the computer. He would then go into administrator profile and change the password. He turned the computer monitor off, to look as though everything was normal.

Whenever we would give him an inch, he would take 10 miles. He turns on charm and innocence to get someone to do what he wants. He will tell our adult children, his friends, and our neighbors we are so unfair to him, because we will not let him on Facebook or on a computer when all his friends are on one.

It's hard to understand what it was like for us unless you have gone through a similar life. We want so much to trust Andy. We did many times, but just when we did, he burned us again. When things were going along well and Andy was not causing trouble, we were able to breathe. But just as I was feeling calm and peaceful, I would pick up my cell phone and notice Andy had changed the settings to suit him and downloaded his explicit songs on my phone.

It took me two hours the last time he did this to figure out how to get the songs off. Scream! I ended up accidently erasing all my contacts. Don't ask me how. It bothers me so much he thinks so little of me to be this disrespectful. If I ask him to take them off he refuses, or he will do something else to my phone. He knows I don't understand how he does it. I change my password often. There must be some hacking information he has.

At the time of this writing Andy is 16. A lot has happened in the past thirteen years.

At 14 he continued to be rude, disrespectful, obstinate, rejecting God, or anyone who truly knew him. He didn't have any friends from school, because he developed a bad reputation by his actions. It was a Christian school with no tolerance for disruption, which is what Andy needed, but didn't want. He wanted to do what he wanted.

He would be disruptive in class, using bad language, giving others a middle finger, or calling them names. When he was about five he gave me the middle finger. I didn't think he knew what it meant then. I tried not to react strongly, but explained it is rude, and not acceptable. He often called me names, too.

He didn't hear that kind of talk at home. Neither his dad, nor I used bad language. I didn't even like "shut-up". A few times in frustration I did say shut-up. His dad used the word "damn", when angry at something he is working on, but rarely. You may think as you read this, why didn't we discipline him and punish him. We did, but nothing affected him

One day he was angry with me for taking him off all electronics. I was standing at my desk in the kitchen with my back towards him. I turned around to find him standing close to me holding a large knife up as if he were going to stab me. He didn't, of course, but just the fact he was thinking about it as far as posturing for it worried me. This was during the time my husband was recovering from surgical complications. My husband did not have any energy to help deal with Andy. Andy was more and more abusive in language to me, refused to help around the house, did not obey house rules, continued to steal our money, lie, and cheat.

We decided to send him to a boys' Christian

therapeutic boarding school for a year. We looked around for months. We finally found one in Missouri. It was close to where my sister lived. It sounded perfect. It was out in the country on a working farm. They would take care of the animals and homeschool as well. There was a river nearby for swimming.

We didn't tell him right away, because we thought he would run away, since he had once, on a freezing cold night. David couldn't help look for him, because he was still recovering from his long stay in the hospital. I went out to look, but ended up calling the local deputies for help. They found him and brought him home.

The day came to take him to the boy's school. It was a long drive, about 18 hours. We told him we were going to visit my sister, which we did. Then we took him to the school. It was one of the hardest things we ever had to do. We love Andy. I cried and prayed all the way back home

My husband John, and I decided to work on our marriage during that year. We started going to a Bible class for married couples our age. It was great. We were able to get to know each other again without arguing over how to discipline

Andy. We didn't always see eye to eye. Occasionally I felt John didn't support me in front of Andy. Our grown children, and their spouses, expressed a difference of opinion on how we should handle Andy, too. For years Caleb would tell us something Andy would do or say that was hard for us to believe, or we didn't want to believe.

The year at the boy's school went fast. He did not progress through the program as they wanted. He was angry with us for sending him away for a year. We tried to tell him it was because I couldn't handle him while dad was not well.

The day came when we ran out of money. So we brought him back home. He decided he would not do anything that resembled work, or if he thought it was, including schoolwork. He told us he should be able to just have fun.

He grew taller, was healthier, and stronger. He was also more confrontational, because he knew he was bigger, and could get away with it. He told us since we sent him to the boys school where he had to work hard every day, he should be able to have fun now.

After Andy returned home, he wanted to listen to explicit music, watch TV, have a cell phone, an Xbox, and eat junk food. He had none of these at the boy's school. I tried to only have good food around, but he would sneak in junk food. He bought a used iPod from a neighbor for $20. Somehow he managed to connect it to our wifi and download explicit music, even though we had a password. He used our credit card to pay for his downloads. A total $170 after he was done. He did not ask us. I was upset. We took the iPod away for a month, during which he had to work to get it back.

When he wants something, he keeps on till he gets it. He will not forget about it. He is deceptive about everything. Later I deleted the music, because we had made a rule against explicit music. He was angry. He doesn't forgive or understand why we do what we do, even after we explain. It's as if he doesn't think he does anything wrong.

We let Andy sign up for a Facebook page. Unknowingly to me his birth mom contacted him. They had some words. At first he didn't know who she was. One day he asked me if so and so was his mom. I answered, "Yes." He started asking for more information. I answered his questions. He posted a question on her page, if she would buy him an X-Box. He would not tell us what else she said to him. We told him she was not legally allowed to contact him. He made comments about going to live with her. We told him after he was older we would try to arrange a meeting with her.

One day I took our four-year-old granddaughter to her gymnastics class. It happened to be next to our bank. Andy went with me. After we arrived, we both went in with our granddaughter. I waited with her until her class started. Andy went outside, and was gone for a long time. He went to our bank without me knowing. He remembered he had a savings account of $2,000. So he went in to try to withdraw some of the money. Of course he couldn't because he was only 16 years old. Even though he could not withdraw any money, the clerk told him there was no money in that account. Andy came back steaming. He wouldn't listen to me explain why. I told him he would still be able to have his money after he turns 18. He would not listen. Everyday, thereafter, he reminded me I spent all his money after sending him away, and he told everyone else, too.

The reality was, yes, I did use his money, because we were struggling financially to pay his tuition of $2,000 a month, which is for a year; then, the next year we had to finish with $1,000 a month. The total for tuition was $3,000 a month. We always planned to put the money back in.

He never listens to reasons and never forgives. Everything is about him. He was jealous of our four-year-old granddaughter. He would be mean to her and say hateful things to me about her, because he knew it would bother me. This was one of his ways to get back at me.

4- REVENGE TIME

We never dreamed the next year, after he came home would be "revenge time." Now, more than ever, he refused to do anything unless he benefited from it. He did not want to go back to the private school he had been in before. We wanted him to go, because we knew he would be lost in a large public school. He started back to the private Christian school in the fall of 2013 after returning home.

The second day we received a call he was cussing at school. He was also picking on some other kids. He complained to us no one liked him or he didn't have any friends. I had thought he was going to start over, be a new person, since we had many conversations about it. Soon he was his old self again. He wouldn't do his homework, or try at school.

We told him if he started trying harder and bring his grades up by the first grading period, we would take him out and let him go to a public school. Before the first report card came out, I guess he knew he was not making passing grades, so he needed something drastic. He didn't say this is why he did what I am about to tell you.

Not only would this year be the year of revenge, it would also be the year of many of my fears coming to fruition. Some days I would just cry, not knowing if I could carry on anymore especially on days when John wasn't feeling good, Andy was causing problems, and our money was running out. God has helped us get through these 13 years; surely, he will help us a little longer. I pray Andy will get a job, move out at 18, and learn to love.

I forgot to tell you the year Andy was gone, Caleb's dog had puppies. I was a pet *Doula* (birth partner) for the mom, and took care of her and the puppies. I loved it. I especially grew attached to one of the puppies named Rocky. He was attached to me, too. He was my friend during the long days I had at home alone. Since I couldn't find a part time job, I stayed home a lot. I would get up in the morning, make my coffee, and sit outside watching the puppies play. All but two of the puppies were sold. Rocky was always my favorite. He was going to be Andy's dog but I ended up taking care of him after Andy returned home.

I was taking care of two big puppies, plus everything else. Andy wouldn't help. He enjoyed playing with the puppies, but that's all.

Dealing with Andy, and trying to help John out when he was tired or in pain was stressful. I'm a nurse, so I naturally took care of John, Andy and Rocky and Rowdy. I loved watching the puppies run and play. They were the best therapy for me. We don't have them now, because of an incident that happened months later which was very traumatic for us. I still miss Rocky very much and cry when I think of him. He would just sit, listen to me talk, and put his head in my lap. God made dogs to comfort us, accept us, play with us, love us, and be by our side no matter what.

In September 2013 after Andy started back to school, we received a call from the principal. Andy was riding his skateboard in the parking lot, had his iPod out during class, and stuck out his middle finger. He kept complaining he hated school, and everyone in it. He was expelled for three days after he texted an inappropriate text to a girl. I think he was trying to get kicked out.

He started going to a local church near our home. We let him even though we were going somewhere else. He seemed happy, making new friends, especially with girls. He ended up talking to one girl a lot on the phone, and going to a movie with her. They broke up. This was the beginning of his many girlfriends.

In November, that dreadful day came when I received a call from John. He said he was at Andy's school, and the school had called the sheriff's department about Andy. I couldn't imagine what he would have done. I prayed all the way there.

When I arrived John took me to a room and said Andy had an iPod, and downloaded pornography on it. I burst out crying, and couldn't stop. We didn't know where he got this new iPod. A detective, and two deputies, had Andy in a room talking to him for an hour. We waited in the next room. Finally they brought us in. I had such mixed feelings. Andy told them he took my credit card, drove my car to Wal-Mart, and bought the $200 iPod. I was shocked. I had not checked my account, so I didn't know $200 was missing, and did not know when he drove the car.

Andy does not have a driver's license. Turns out he drove my car around 10:30 at night. John and I had gone to bed early. After he had bought this iPod, he would stand outside a neighbor's house to access their wifi so he could download what he wanted. It was usually something explicit

5- Addictions

Our wireless modem was not working. I suspected Andy was trying to change the settings or get the password; because one minute it was working, the next it wasn't. I had seen Andy at the computer. He would not tell me what he was doing. We started using land connection through the telephone jack. We have kept it that way, hoping it would be safer. Andy has locked out my cell phone by trying to figure out my password by entering it too many times. I was on our house phone for an hour trying to restore it with the telephone company.

The detective kept Andy's newer iPod for evidence. After this incident Andy was expelled and stayed home for six weeks till I could get him in another school. I tried several alternative schools, but they would not accept Andy for various reasons. He would just lie around watching movies on the DVD player, since we do not have TV. I was nervous about him going to another school. I didn't want him doing the same thing again. He had not been convicted of anything yet. Andy had told us he would work hard if we let him go to a public school.

We finally received all the information needed to sign him up for a local public high school. He liked the new school. It was a sea of potential friends. He was able to hide better. There was always another gullible new friend. I know I sound cynical, but it is all the truth. It was nice to see him happy though with new friends; but I held my breath, because something would eventually happen, and then he would be on to a new friend. I have been burned; so I know. I have learned not to believe anything he says, and not to trust him. As soon as I would turn my back he would look in my purse for money, credit card, or car keys. We hide our keys, money, and debit cards now. There were times I went to the grocery store, bought a cart full of food, went through the check out and remembered I left my debit card at home hidden somewhere. I have had to get a new debit card three times this year. Our bank probably thinks I'm the most scattered brain woman.

Andy took my husband's work phone once searching and accessing porn. My husband John, told him that could get him fired, because it is a company phone. As far as I know, he hasn't done it again. Andy did talk a friend at school into giving him an old phone that he could connect to wifi at school, which he used during school everyday. On one occasion the principal saw him, and told him to give it to him. Andy refused and put it in his sock. The principal called my husband, John, who went to the school. John called me. We told the principal if need be, to call the sheriff. Andy gave his phone to a friend. The friend turned it in per principal request. Sure enough, after we looked at it, he had pornography on it. I hate pornography, how it grabs a hold of a boy and won't let go. We tried to get Andy into sports or working out, but he refuses to. We took the phone away. So far Andy was making failing grades. The teachers tried to help him, the guidance counselor, and others, but he did not try. He would not tell anyone why.

In the mean time we have been going to court once a month and started seeing a psychologist. It's a process, to get a lawyer, then go to court to hear from the lawyer once a month, and for the accused to stand before the judge to find out the next court date. I never thought John and I would be sitting in the courtroom with people from all walks of life, as they were being accused of some crime. It was an uncomfortable feeling. We both were feeling sorry for all these people. Many of them must have had a difficult upbringing, and were not able to break the cycle of making bad decisions. Most of them did not look healthy, were not dressed appropriately, or looked dirty.

As of this writing we have not gone to trial yet. We don't have a date. We are scheduled for another hearing for Andy to make a plea. Andy doesn't have much to say about it. He says it is the private school's fault, because they all hate him. I said, "No, you make your own decisions." He committed a felony on the lower end of the scale. It wasn't considered a felony years ago, but it is now. He put an iPod on video and set it up on the paper towel dispenser in the girl's bathroom at school. He was dared to. The boy who dared him also said if Andy did it he would be expelled. Afterwards, he took it out and showed it to a couple boys, then deleted it. They told the teacher. Some of the boys at school had sisters there. They were angry and beat Andy up, but not seriously. He still has not said he was sorry or shown any remorse. I think he wanted to be expelled. He made a lot of enemies that day.

If that had been someone else's son putting a video in the restroom where my daughter went to school, I would be just as angry as everyone there, and would want the boy expelled. I understand how they feel, and I want Andy to be punished for that. The school had an obligation to call the sheriff. It would have been irresponsible not to. It was difficult for John and I to have to go up to the school, to face everyone we knew and had good relationships with. It felt like a bad dream. John and I are Christians, responsible citizens, obey the law, and help others in need. Andy has not learned from our example and teachings. You may be thinking we were hard, or authoritarian, but we weren't. We may have been too permissive if anything. We have always surrounded him with good honest people, and he has had good friends, but he lost those friends after he stole from them. Andy takes; but does not give back, unless he wants something in return.

We have always wanted to give Andy the benefit of a doubt, but often regretted it later. So many things have happened over the years that I could write forever to tell you. One of the reasons for writing now is to tell couples thinking about adopting to look very closely at themselves, ask questions about the child's background, and the birth parents.

It sounds harsh or cold to not want a child who may have been severely abused, or never attached. I believe a couple considering adopting an older child will need to determine if they are strong enough in their relationship, in disciplining, and wisdom. Love is not enough. We found that out the hard way.

We love children, have big hearts, a big house, and live in the country. Protecting our biological children is important, too. When I think about how Caleb was always so happy, healthy, easygoing, and lovable when he was nine, it makes me cry with sadness that he suffered. After Andy came, Caleb began eating more, gained weight, and started having angry outbursts. He didn't want to go anywhere with us if Andy was in the car. Some of it was our fault we didn't know how to handle everything. We tried hard, to help them be friends, but with no success.

Caleb had not wanted us to adopt Andy. John and I failed to be there for Caleb. Parents need to be strong, assertive, a responder not a reactor, to take charge, to be patient, and loving. I'm not saying perfect, but make sure they are both responders to what life brings them. John is "laid back" and I came from a home with an alcoholic dad.

Our son, Jay, who is in his twenties, his wife, and their one year old moved here from Denver. Our son had taken an interest in Andy. He wanted to spend time with him. They hung out as much as possible. We were hoping and praying it would be good for Andy and help him make better decisions. Jay began to see Andy couldn't be trusted and was out to get what he could get. I was sorry he had to be burned, too.

I had hoped Andy would feel better and start caring about someone else. He has a big wall up. Love cannot get in or out. The only time he ever uttered the words "I love you" was when he was at the therapeutic boys' boarding school when we would talk to him on the phone. His mentor was next to him to make sure he didn't tell us lies so we would come get him. The mentor may have told him to tell us that, after we said it to him.

6- REACTIVE ATTACHMENT DISORDER OR PSYCHOPATH?

One day in 2014, our son Jay mentioned in passing he thought Andy acted like a psychopath. Later that day I looked up the definition. Wow, it sounded just like Andy. If a child does not learn to attach to a loving adult from birth they are more likely to develop social problems such as being a sociopath or psychopath. These two words basically mean the same. When you think of psychopath what is the first thought that comes to your mind? Violence? Yes, that's what I would have thought, too. But to be a psychopath doesn't mean you have to be physically abusive, or to have killed someone, but there is a possibility of it becoming that way. Below are some of the characteristics according to Dr. Robert Hare. Many other sources of information I have found list these same qualities.

Aggressive narcissism Glibness/superficial charm Grandiose sense of self-worth Pathological lying Lack of remorse or guilt Shallow affect (genuine emotion is short lived) Callousness; lack of empathy Failure to accept responsibility for own actions Need for stimulation Impulsivity Juvenile delinquency May be violent Poor behavioral control

Andy has all of these. Some of them he has had since three years of age, such as, lack of remorse, need for constant stimulation, impulsiveness, and lying. He never seemed to understand why lying and stealing is wrong, or why he should be respectful of others. Some of these traits can be treated with therapy and possibly medication if started early, way before the teen years. Once they hit the teen years, they will not be cooperative. Andy refuses to see any counselors since we met with a psychologist. He will be 17 years old next month.

None of the therapist, physicians, or counselors we have seen over the years, nor the ADHD clinic where he was evaluated and tested, have ever mentioned this possibility. Sociopath is a very strong word. No one wants to suggest this is his problem, because of our past knowledge of it. Serial killers have been sociopaths, but not all sociopaths are serial killers.

A parent will probably deny their child could be a sociopath because of serial killers. There hasn't been a definitive way to test for a psychopath diagnosis. A psychopath can lie through the whole test or talk the tester into believing he didn't need it. After Andy committed the felony at the private school, the deputies took him to the Sheriff's office to be fingerprinted, take a DNA sample, and a mug shot. Andy agreed to see a psychologist. The psychologist wasn't able to help us except to advise us. We saw him about four or five times. At the last appointment when we were alone, I asked him if he thought Andy had the signs of a sociopath. He nodded his head yes, and said, "There is no way to test for it under 18 years of age." If he has all the symptoms, all the time, wouldn't that mean something?

Why is he being tried in court as an adult? Isn't 18 years old considered an adult? He can't vote until he is 18. He can't buy alcohol till 21. Our kids are exposed to sex 24/7; but if they peep at someone undressing, they are charged with a felony. A misdemeanor is more understandable for a first offense. We learned that both of the possible charges for Andy have the same punishment. It doesn't make sense to me.

When a child has traits of a psychopath, it is called RAD. When an adult has them, it is called psychopath or sociopath. A study put out by the University of Nevada states: *Reactive Attachment Disorder (RAD) is any disruption in the attachment process resulting in a child's failure to form a SECURE bond/attachment with a parental figure (Bowlby, 1988). Secure attachment forms when a child's physical and emotional needs are consistently met, especially during the first two years of life.*

My mind is whirling around with more and more thoughts coming to mind that I want to write about, but I'm not able to find the words. So much is still happening since Andy has joined our family. I love him so much, but he won't let us in. He has always pushed everyone away since he was two. I'm thankful John and I are still married. It has taken a toll on us, especially with John's continued physical health issues. We don't always see eye to eye when it comes to Andy. We are committed to each other and know someday it will get better, hopefully before we retire. RAD has many of the traits as psychopath, or should I say social disorder.

An example of his behavior was, all the time while John was in the hospital, at home ill and out of work for six months in 2012, Andy never once asked how he was doing, or expressed any concern? He would only ask for money or things. Andy was 14. John had been in intensive care about four times, once on a respirator, and his body swelled up with fluids. He was kept in a light coma.

When I was at home, Andy didn't react to my sadness. It was as if nothing out of the ordinary was going on. I would visit my husband everyday, so we asked Caleb to stay with Andy. He didn't want to, but he did.

We kept giving Andy chance after chance after chance, thinking he would be more responsible the next time. He can be charming and appear honest, but he isn't. Finally after 13 years, I have learned to never trust him. I don't believe anything he says. Part of the reason we kept thinking maybe he has changed is because we cannot comprehend his thinking. We have a conscience, we love, trust, give, and respect others' privacy. We don't understand how it is possible to **not** have a conscience.

One day in early spring this year 2014, Andy missed his bus for school. He told me he texted a neighbor who said they would take him to school. Andy was being so calm and sweet. He said "Thanks Mom," after I made him breakfast. I watched him go out the door and into the neighbors yard. I turned around and started cleaning up the kitchen. I believed him.

After an hour or two, my daughter called me and said she saw Andy riding his skateboard in a store parking lot. She told me where he was. I called the sheriff's office to pick him up since he was skipping school. They called back and said they had him. They asked me to meet them. I did and proceeded to take him to school. It was around 11 AM. On the way to school Andy said he needed his book bag. I went home so he could get it. He went upstairs and locked himself in his room and refused to come out. When I'm alone with him, I try not to make him too angry. He is intimidating to me sometimes. He has never hit me, but he gets very angry and cusses.

Do you remember Scott Peterson who killed his eight months pregnant wife? In an article on crimelibrary.com he was described by this statement, *"He seems an obvious sociopath now, but for a while he'd had good luck in convincing women that he was a sweet, serious and loving guy. That he was too good to be true."*

Earlier this year, Andy and another boy from school had arranged to meet a girl after school. Whichever one was able to meet her first, would be the one to have sex with her. After school that day Andy came home acting stranger than usual. He told me he was going to a friend's house to play video games. I told him I would take him. He said he would ride his bike there. I said I would feel more comfortable driving him in the car, and asked where the boy lived. He wouldn't tell me. I don't remember all the details, but he ended up taking off when I wasn't watching.

Sometimes he would take off without telling us and come back later. We stopped calling the sheriff every time Andy was gone. It's difficult to have to watch a 16 year old as closely as a 16 month old.

Later that night I received a call I never wanted to get. A man said Andy was at his house and was caught having sex with his daughter. This can't be happening. I am a person who always follows rules, and want to do the right thing. I didn't know what to say.

I called outside to John who was working in the yard. I'm so glad he was home. We went over to pick up Andy. When we arrived we saw Andy's bike in the yard. Inside we found the girl in one chair with her face in her hands, Andy on the couch looking at the floor, and the parents standing in the middle of the room.

They said their daughter was just as guilty for arranging the meeting with Andy, so they didn't fully blame him. I prayed the girl would not become pregnant. We talked to Andy, but he doesn't seem to listen. He never apologized to us, but he did to her parents after we told him to. It's been six months, so guess she isn't.

The next day I couldn't find my debit card. I searched and searched. Couldn't figure out what I did with it. The following day a friend of Andy's happened to be in the grocery store when the cashier was showing the lost card to the manager. The friend saw the name on it. She told them she knew us and would call us.

She did. We went to pick it up. Andy had taken it to buy a monster drink on his bicycle ride to the house two days before and left it.

Andy met another girl from school. She was fourteen. They talked constantly into the morning hours. In one month the number of text messages on his phone would be in the three thousands. Andy told her he loved her. He talked to her on his speaker phone while in his room. She would listen to Andy play his video games, and you could hear her dog in the background. She would yell at the dog. It was cute. She began to come over and I had to keep a close eye on them.

They wanted to go up to his bedroom and lay on the bed. I told them to leave the door open. I had to call up or go up to check on them. Once I went up to check on them, and he had his hand under her shirt. I said, "Take your hand out and come downstairs." They dated for a while going back and forth, till suddenly they stopped.

Andy was on to another girl now. In the beginning he and his new friend started talking on the bus, then talking on the phone, then to arranging a meeting. I heard him say to her he loved her. The girl was a neighbor. She walked over once and I met her. I warned her Andy could be charming when he wanted something. She told him. Of course he was angry with me.

They hung out more and more. One evening Andy was at her house when her parents were there. They were fond of Andy. He was fun and cute. Andy came home after eating supper with them about 7 PM. John and I went to bed about 9:30 PM. Andy was getting ready for bed. We went to sleep.

At 5 AM the following morning I noticed Andy's light was on. I knocked on the door and asked why he was up. He said he just got home from his girlfriend's house. This part was the truth. I was shocked. He told me they both fell asleep at her house while they were watching *Forest Gump*. This part is somewhat true. I asked if her parents were watching it, too. He said, "No." I asked, "Why didn't you come home when you were getting sleepy?" He said he fell asleep fast. I had my doubts. I told him I would have to tell her parents if they didn't know about this. They should know since it is their house and their daughter.

I knew they lived near us. As I was driving down the road they lived on I met an older woman on a golf cart like the one Andy's girlfriend drove around in the neighborhood. I stopped and asked her if she knew her. She said yes, she was her grandmother. She gave me a phone number for her parents. That evening the mom and daughter came over. The dad was still at work. The story that came out was after her parents went to bed the daughter unlocked the door so Andy could come back in about 10 PM. He stayed till 5 AM. Her parents were livid. The parents broke off the relationship, which is a good thing.

Now Andy is after another girl. They talk nonstop on their cell phones. Andy does not have picture or video messaging. He only has texting and phone calling. I can hear him talking all hours of the night when I wake up. He tells her he loves her. Usually, I get up at 5 AM and will hear him talking on the phone with a girl, since he has it on speakerphone. I will tell him to hang up. I have heard the girl's name, but have never met her.

Just a few days ago Andy was cleaning his

room. He brought a container down with trash. I happened to look in it when he quickly covered something up. I asked, "What's that?" I moved the paper and saw a condom wrapper. I asked if it was the girl he's been talking to. He said no, that we didn't know who she was. I explained how he could get sexually transmitted diseases, AIDS, and get a girl pregnant, even with a condom. He said at least he was being safe. I said they are not 100% effective, only 98-99%. He argues, of course. What do I know? I'm only 56 years old. I have to say if he is going to be sexually active, I am glad he used the condom.

He has always been resourceful, and street-smart like. As a toddler he wanted to be his own boss. He wasn't afraid of anything, anyone, or the dark. When he was younger I tried to instill a little healthy fear, such as not leaving my side when we were in public, not talking to strangers, or walking out in the street alone. He acted as though he already knew everything, and still does.

I have wanted so much to love him, but he hasn't let me in. I wish I knew then when we first adopted him about RAD being a big possibility and the traits a child would have with the Attachment Disorder, maybe we could have been more aggressive to address that. I knew a little about detachment disorder, but didn't know enough to look into it.

I do not want to spend any more of our other children and grandchildren's inheritance money on Andy. We have spent more than $30,000 (not including what he stole from us). We also have been paying for him to go to a private school. We were glad in that respect to put him in a public school to relieve us of the $250 a-month-tuition. If he is not going to change or respond to discipline or punishment, we might as well not keep paying for it. We pray everyday for him.

One reason why we put him in a Christian Private School was hoping the love and teaching from the Bible would be instilled in him, and new a smaller classroom would help him learn. He knows the teachings, but is 100% against it all. He doesn't realize that living in a life of hate, bitterness, drugs, alcohol is as much being a slave as what he thinks of having to obey God. He doesn't want to have to do what God says, yet he is doing what Satan says.

Presently, we are financially struggling. John has health issues from his surgery. He has abdominal pain, low energy, and has to be on a special diet. We don't have the money to go to holistic or integrative physicians who don't take insurance. Other physicians don't know what is causing his pain. He has been to a gastroenterologist but to no avail. Six months ago he lost 20 pounds in six weeks before we changed his diet.

We thought as long as Andy was in a safe home with loving and caring parents, the bonding would come. It didn't. No one said anything about how to help him learn attachment. I don't remember much in our foster parenting classes or adoption counseling. It would have been good to learn about this early on, what the characteristics were to watch for and to treat accordingly.

Andy had a friend over to spend the night last week. This boy has been tolerant of Andy, and does pretty much what Andy wants. I woke up and heard them talking at 5 AM. They were making noises, and then I heard one of them go into the bathroom and throw up, while the other one was laughing. One of them took a shower, and went back to bed. I didn't know who it was. We let them sleep. It's better that way.

Later, after they were up, I asked Andy who threw up and why. He said he did, because he ate too many *Oreos*. I believed him. I don't know why I did. I told my husband John what had happened. He said he found a few small bottles of alcohol in our yard that must have been thrown out Andy's upstairs window. I asked Andy how he got them. My bad. He said he stole them from the ABC store. That seemed strange that they would let a teenager come in, walk around, and then just walk back out. I don't know why I even bother to ask him any questions, since he doesn't give honest answers.

As a Mom I want to know what he is up to. He says he is his own person and we have no business in his business. We tell him as long as he is under our roof he should follow certain rules of respect and honesty.

We use money as a reward or punishment. If he has been hateful to me, I will not give him any money to see a movie. If he isn't helping around the house, I will not give him money for soda or a candy bar. I he wants soda or candy he borrows money from friends. I'm not sure if he pays them back. He has earned some money by working for our oldest son a few times. He spends his money on monster drinks, sodas, candy, or a pen that is like an e-cigarette that has a flavored smoke with a little nicotine. It is supposedly not as toxic as cigarettes. I have my doubts. Not sure how he is getting these either. One thing I can say about him is he is resourceful. He doesn't stop till he gets what it is he wants. If only he would use that quality for good.

I want to explain more what happens when we give him an inch, he takes a mile. For example, Andy and I were having a good morning. When he thinks I'm in a good mood, he will ask me for things we have said no to in the past. One day some visitors stopped by. We were all talking and laughing. All of a sudden Andy comes out with "we should get wireless wifi." He smiles a cute smile. I'm thinking,

"Where did that come from. He must have thought I would say yes." (John and I decided, until he leaves home we will not pay to have wireless Internet again.) It must have seemed I was vulnerable to say yes to him, because I was in a pleasant and agreeable mood. He took advantage of the situation, but he still heard a "no" answer.

He continues to keep asking us for wireless Internet. He will not tell us his real reason. I think it is so he can hack into it to access wifi for his Xbox. He told me he knows how to hack into our neighbor's wifi. Not sure why he told me that. Guess it was in one of his weak moments. He has an Xbox now for the summer to keep him busy. He did some yard work for John to earn the use back. If he steals my debit card again and uses it to download games or movies to his Xbox, I might just throw it out his upstairs window.

7- OUR COURT PROCEEDINGS

We thought July 21, 2014 would be the day Andy would have his trial. We arrived early and sat in the big courtroom. There was a judge sitting at the bench, a stenographer was in the front of the room and about four deputies were standing against a wall. There were a few more people sitting in the bench seats where we were sitting. Andy's lawyer ushered us out to a private conference room. He told Andy he had two choices. He could accept the guilty plea of felony and receive his sentence of community work, or refuse and plea to a misdemeanor. The punishments were the same. The felony would follow him forever and interfere with getting a job. North Carolina organizes felony crimes into 10 different lettered categories, from Class A to I, with Class B felonies further divided into Class B1 and Class B2. Class A felonies are the most serious crimes a person can commit, while Class 1 felonies are considered the least serious type of felony offense. Andy's is in the Class 1 range.

Sentences depend on if there is a prior record. Andy does not have a record, so he would not do jail time, this time. With each conviction points accrue. These points add up to determine sentencing. If this felony holds up, and Andy commits another felony, he would serve some jail time, because he would have gotten many points.

If the district attorney accepts the plea for a misdemeanor, Andy will not stand trial. If they refuse, Andy will stand trial and have witnesses from the private school he was expelled from. This would be very uncomfortable to all of us.

We asked Andy's lawyer if the Judge would require Andy to finish high school and receive counseling as part of his punishment. We knew Andy would not do this on his own or by our prompting.

Andy signed the refusal to accept the felony charge. Now we have another court date set for in September to go back to find out if the District Attorney will accept this or not. Our lawyer said he would talk to the District Attorney's office to get them to accept the refusal and charge Andy with a misdemeanor instead, since he is only 16 and this is his first offence. That works for us. To think of Andy having to go through life with a felony over his head and having to register as a sex offender was overwhelming. I just couldn't believe this was really happening. It was as if it was all a dream.

Yesterday I picked up one of Andy's friends to come spend the night. It was about 5:15 PM. I brought them back home. I dressed for my Jazzercise class, which is just down the street from my house. I was driving my husband John's truck since my car is in the shop. As I was getting ready Andy said he and his friend were going to go check out an abandoned house that was very close to the church building where my class was being held. They left before I did and started walking down our road. I drove my husband's truck and passed them on the way to my class. Twenty minutes into my aerobics class, Andy comes in. There were probably 10 women in the room with me. I was on the far side of the room. He comes over to me and asks for the truck keys to drive to the abandoned house to load up some stuff they found inside. I said, "NO." My purse was close by against a wall, so he walks over to it to find the keys. (He doesn't have a driver's license). He said, "The house isn't far away." I said no again. (In my mind I know a lot can happen if he drives a truck down the street onto a busy road, and besides it's against the law). He wasn't giving up, so I picked up my purse and left, so he would follow me out the door. I drove the truck home and left them to walk. Now that I think about it he must have had this plan in his mind all along. That may be why he told me they were going to the abandoned house near my Jazzercise class.

When I looked at pictures of Andy when he was young, he looks so sweet and innocent. I wondered what Andy's life would be like as an adult. I fear he will not concentrate on anything but sexual gratification, because he is craving it now. We try to impress on him there is more to life than sex and that hard work can be rewarding. To have a friend he will need to be one, and to care about someone other than himself. If indeed he is a *psychopath,* anything we say will not stick or make sense to him. I want to warn other people to be on their guard around him. More importantly to warn girls, not to let his charm and compliments fool them into thinking he really cares.

I don't know if there is hope for Andy or the rest of our family, but I do have a little hope left. I know God can still work miracles. In our human minds we discount miracles sometimes, because of our experiences. We are not assured of a life without pain. We are assured of a way to deal with the pain, if we depend on God to help us through. We may try to handle everything ourselves, but realize we are not able to. I will ask Him to please take care of everything and help us through it.

When I look back at the past 13 years, it's amazing to me we still have some sanity left. I am more *attention deficit* than I used to be. I know we could not have made it this far, if we didn't have faith in Jesus Christ. I wish I knew what the future holds. Well maybe not. Taking one day at a time is best. I know God won't give me more than I can handle, but it sure gets awfully close some times. I fall down on my knees and pray. I'm trying to remember the blessings, but it's hard when I know our son Caleb is struggling with his hurt and pain from when he was living through all of this too. I feel we neglected him since we trusted him to take care of himself.

CONCLUSION

This past month I began therapy to sort out all the emotions I am going through since Andy left home three months ago in October 2014, to live with his birth family, and the guilt I have concerning Caleb. I commented to my therapist, that none of Andy's counselors or physicians ever discussed Andy's oppositional defiance diagnosis. She said, "That is because no one knows what to do about it."

I'm studying to become certified as an aromatherapy nurse this year. Pure essential oils are used to treat many conditions such as headaches, sore muscles, swelling, cuts, depression, and anxiety. The limbic system in our brain has a structure called the Amygdala. It stores traumatic emotions and is closely connected to the olfactory system. Pure grade essential aromatic oils are able to cross the blood brain barrier thus reaching the Amygdala. This may help to release pent up emotions a child may have from neglect or abuse. It is worth trying while your child is young, and hopefully help your child deal with those emotions. You may contact me or find a certified aromatherapist near you.

If Andy was younger again, I would certainly use the oils with him and take him to a psychotherapist.

There was a lot we didn't know before we adopted. With this book I want to help you to understand that adoption isn't all a rosy picture. Know your strengths and weaknesses. You need to know the hard realities, too. Protect your biological children. Then if you choose to adopt, you will go in with your eyes wide open, and you can't say, "Why didn't anyone tell us?"

RESOURCES

http://www.attach.org
http://www.crimelibrary.com/notorious_murd
ers/family/laci_peterson/11.html Amazon.com

Dr. Gabor Mate is author of *Scattered: How Attention Deficit Disorder Originates and What You Can Do About It* (I don't agree with all his opinions of America, or his philosophies, but I believe he has his facts straight. I have thought for a long time ADHD could be prevented. Maybe not all the time, but some of the time.) On Amazon.com

http://www.lovefraud.com Five books I have read in the past few months are listed on the next page.

1. *WithoutConscience*byRobertD.Hare,PhDpublish
    edin1999by Guilford Press,

2. *TheSociopathNextDoor*byMarthaStout,PhDpubli
    shedin2005 by Harmony Books.

3. *WhenLoveisNotEnough*byCherryWilloughby,Kin
    dleEbookon Amazon.com

4. *Surviving Evil* by Junie Moon, Kindle ebook on Amazon.com

5. *Detached: Surviving Reactive Attachment Disorder* by Jessie Hogsett, Kindle Ebook on Amazon.com

Below is a study I found recently after writing this book. It is interesting to note the Amygdala gland in the limbic system that stores emotional trauma.

https://www.med.uvm.edu/ahec/downloads/School_Nurse_GrandroundsJan10.p df

From my studies in aromatherapy some oils such as Frankincense may be able to release the emotional trauma stored in the Amygdala. If Andy was three years old again, I would use the oils to try to help him. It is worth a try. The oils would not hurt him unless I went overboard. The oils can be used in a diffuser in the child's room or applied diluted to the bottom of the feet and on the back of neck. Consistent use with pure grade essential oils is needed in order to benefit from them.

ABOUT THE AUTHOR

Lynn Pike

Registered Nurse since 1979. Worked 17 years in different medical fields. 14 of those years were in mother/baby. When my husband and I began having children, I did not work outside the home for 12 years. I love to listen to self-help/motivation audio books in my car and teaching others.

Facebook.com/pages/whydidnttheytellus

www.ingramcontent.com/pod-product-compliance
Lightning Source LLC
Chambersburg PA
CBHW060658030426
42337CB00017B/2673

* 9 7 8 0 6 9 2 2 6 4 3 3 1 *